D1203159

Easy to Read! • Easy to Draw!

Cars and Trucks

With many thanks to Debbie Guy-Christiansen, Rosanne Guararra, Jane O'Connor, and Diane Picard—JH

8-20-03

ISBN: 0-8431-4547-1   A B C D E F G H I J

Cars and Trucks

By Joan Holub

Illustrated by
Joan Holub and Dana Regan

PSS!
PRICE STERN SLOAN

Big and little.
Fast and slow.
Cars and trucks
are on the go.

Cars that zoom.
Trucks that haul.
I'll show you how
to draw them all!

On city streets,
the sweepers sweep.

Use these shapes to draw a street sweeper.

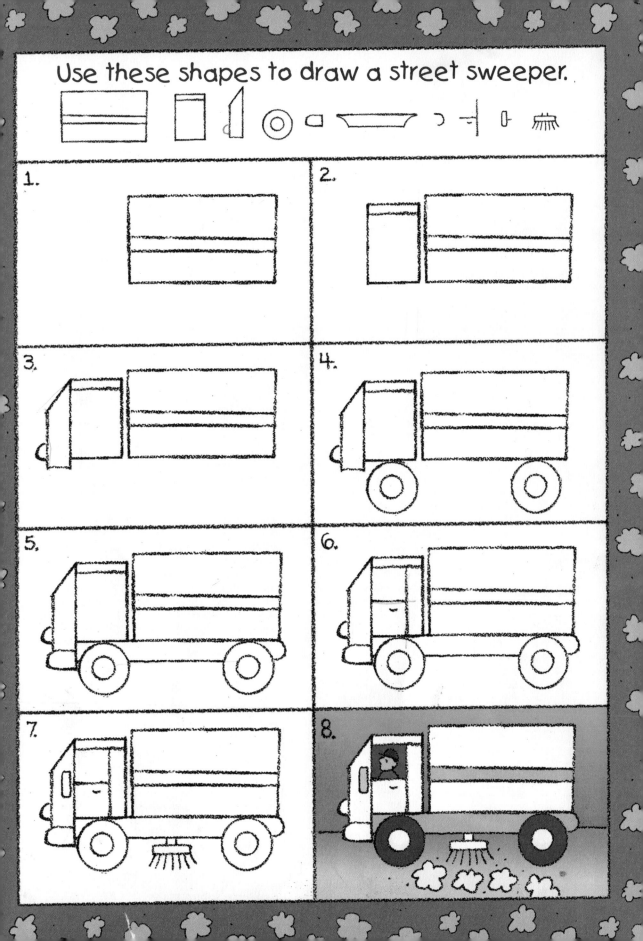

And taxicabs go
Beep! Beep! Beep!

Use these shapes to draw a taxicab.

1.

2.

3.

4.

5.

6.

7.

8.

9.

TAXI

TAXI

TAXI

TAXI

When you hear
loud sirens blast.
An ambulance
is rushing past.

Use these shapes to draw an ambulance.

1.

2.

3.

4.

5.

6.

7.

8.

Ambulance

This fire truck has
a ladder and hose.

Use these shapes to draw a fire truck.

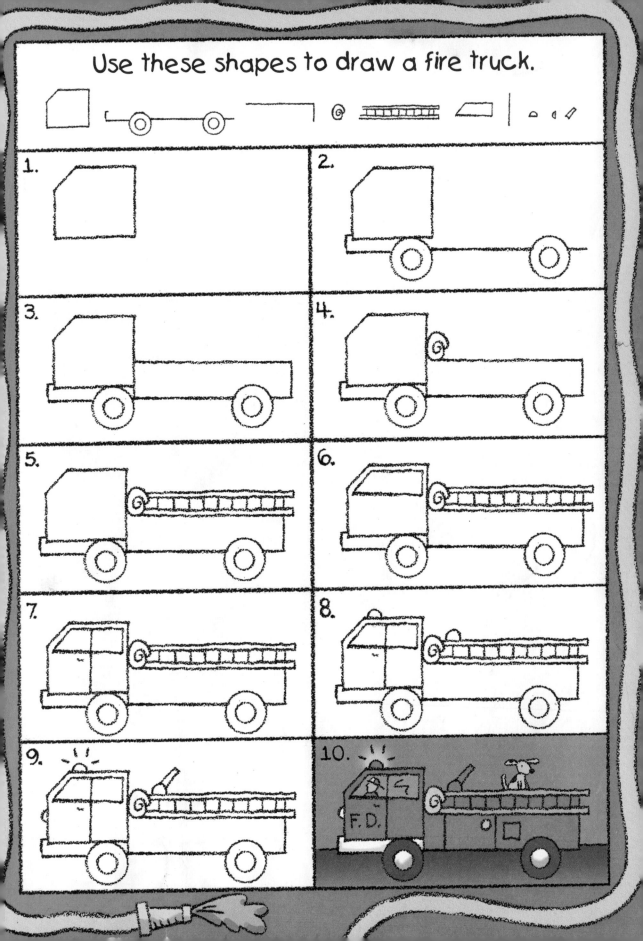

1.

2.

3.

4.

5.

6.

7.

8.

9.

10.

F.D.

Snowplows clear paths
when it snows.

Use these shapes to draw a snowplow.

1.

2.

3.

4.

5.

6.

7.

8.

9.

10.

A garbage truck
picks up the trash.

Use these shapes to draw a garbage truck.

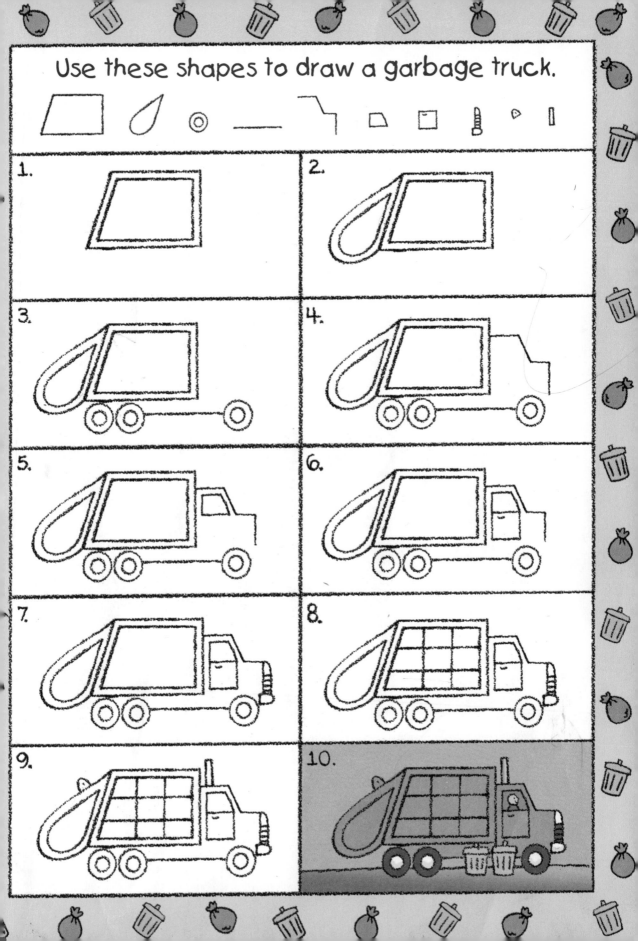

When trouble calls,
police cars dash.

Use these shapes to draw a police car.

1.

2.

3.

4.

5.

6.

7.

8.

9.

POLICE

Someone's building.
Crash! Bang! Boom!
Trucks are helping.
Vroom! Vroom! Vroom!

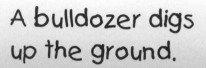

A bulldozer digs
up the ground.

Use these shapes to draw a bulldozer.

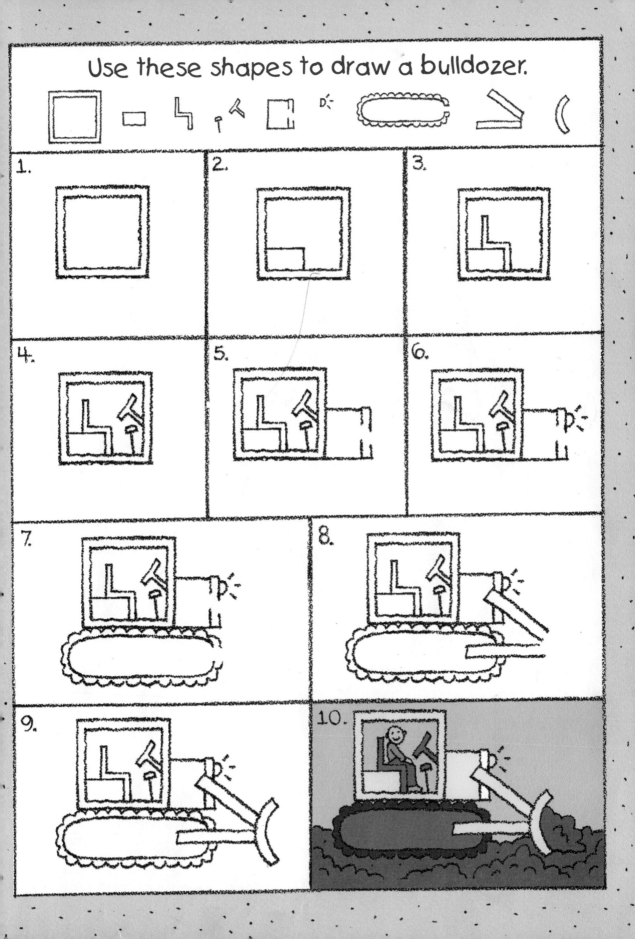

A cement mixer goes
round and round.

Use these shapes to draw a cement mixer.

1.

2.

3.

4.

5.

6.

7.

8.

9.

10.

A dump truck dumps
a heavy load.

Use these shapes to draw a dump truck.

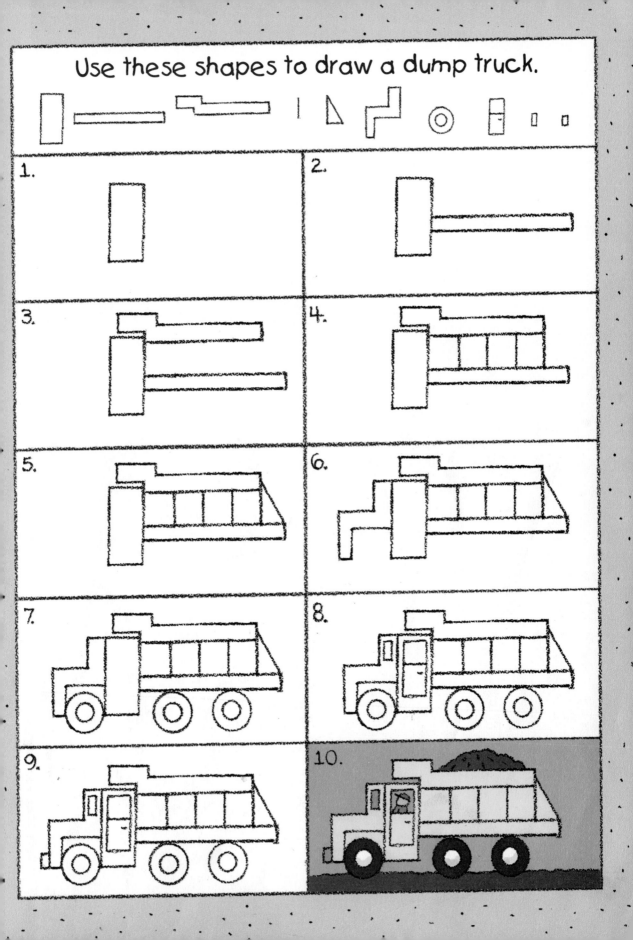

A steamroller
paves the road.

Use these shapes to draw a steamroller.

1.

2.

3.

4.

5.

6.

7.

8.

Eighteen wheelers
are big and strong.
They carry loads
and zoom along.

Use these shapes to draw an eighteen wheeler.

1.

2.

3.

4.

5.

6.

7.

8.

9.

HWY

Wave the flag.
A race begins.
Around the track!
Your race car wins!

Use these shapes to draw a race car.

1.

2.

3.

4.

5.

6.

7.

8.

9.

GO!

One race car spins,
and it gets stuck.
Quick — let's help!
Draw a tow truck!

Use these shapes to draw a tow truck.

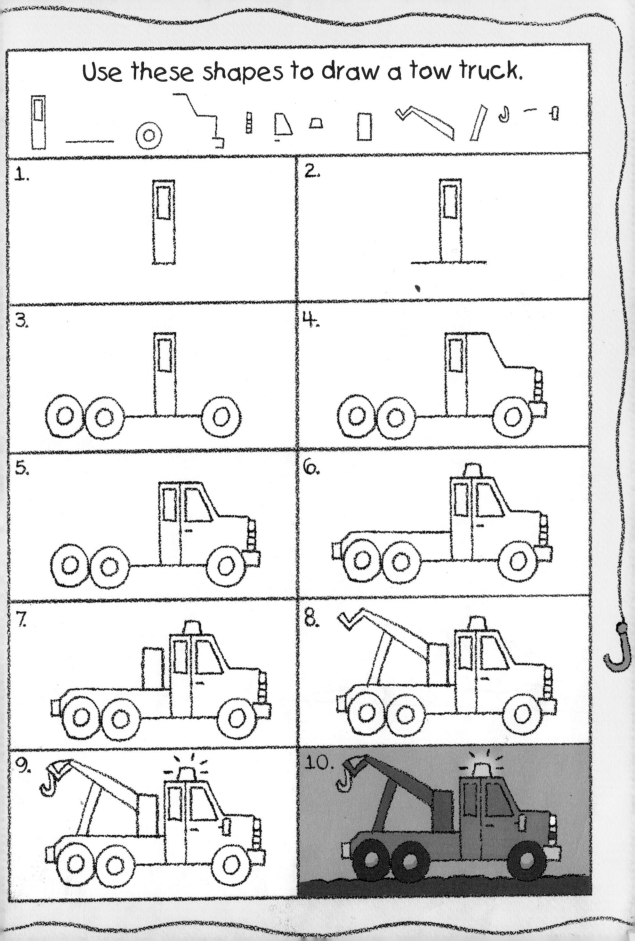

1.

2.

3.

4.

5.

6.

7.

8.

9.

10.

On the farm,
the trucks work hard
in the fields
and the barnyard.

A farmer's pickup
herds the cows.

Use these shapes to draw a pickup truck.

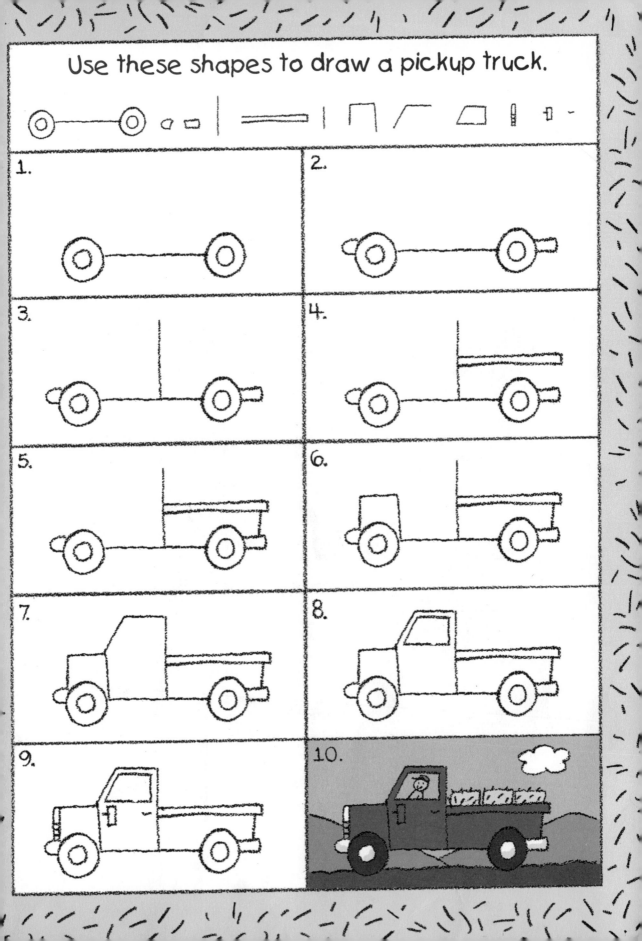

1.

2.

3.

4.

5.

6.

7.

8.

9.

10.

Seeds go in rows
the tractor plows.

Use these shapes to draw a tractor.

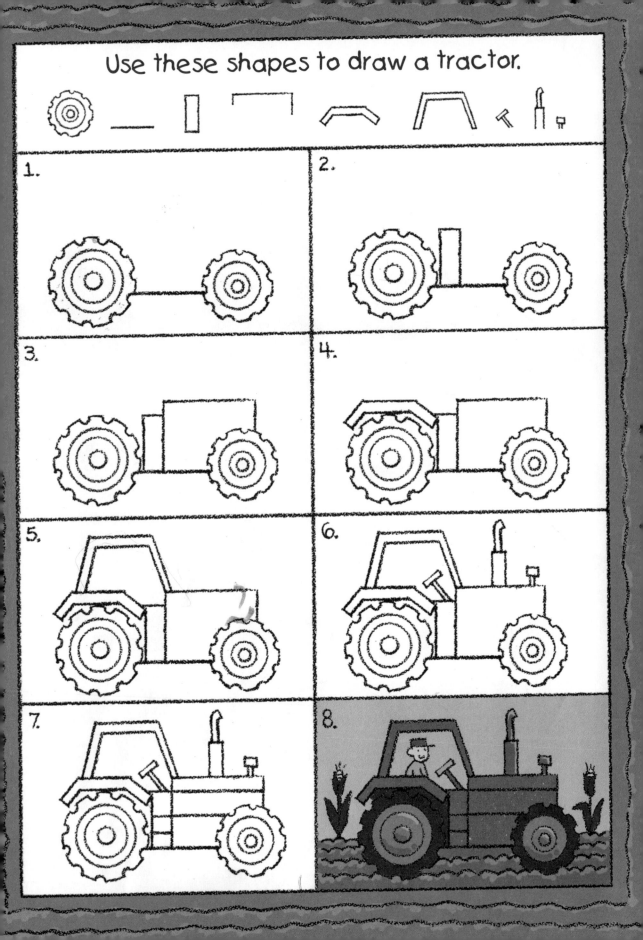

1.

2.

3.

4.

5.

6.

7.

8.

The mail truck brings mail
with every trip.

Use these shapes to draw a mail truck.

1.

2.

3.

4.

5.

6.

7.

8. MAIL

The ice-cream truck
sells a double-dip.

Use these shapes to draw an ice-cream truck.

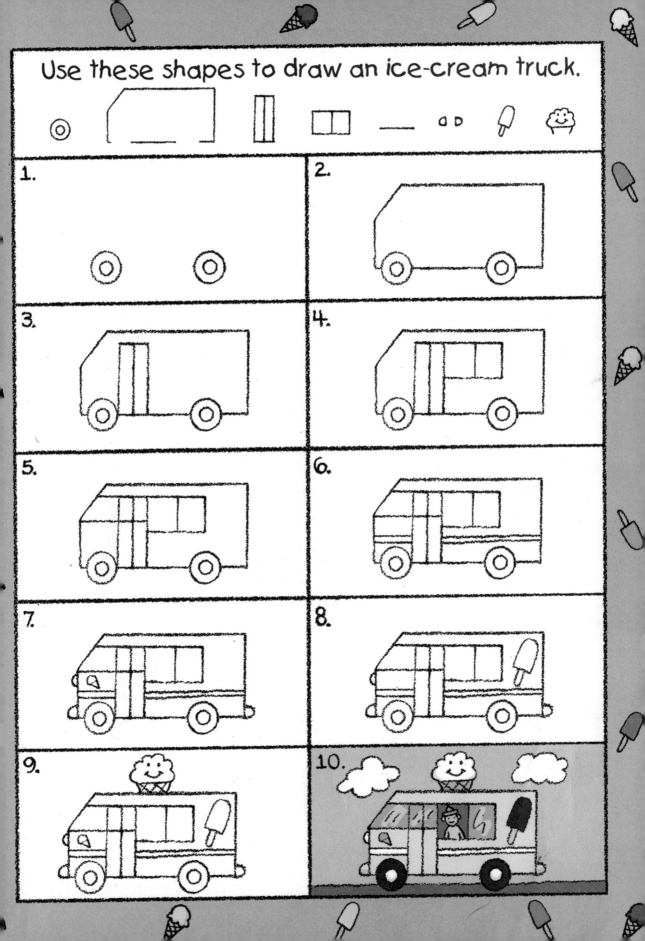

1.

2.

3.

4.

5.

6.

7.

8.

9.

10.

A bus takes kids
like me to school . . .

Use these shapes to draw a school bus.

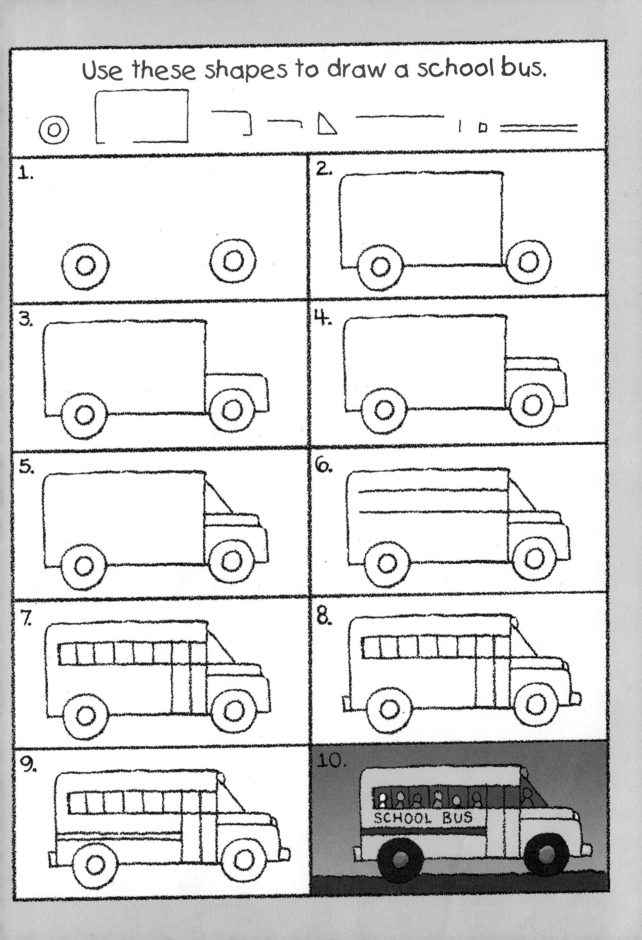

1.

2.

3.

4.

5.

6.

7.

8.

9.

10. SCHOOL BUS

We learn to draw.
Drawing is cool!